The
Criminal Advocate's
Survival Guide

by

Jan Davies

Carbolic Smoke Ball Co.
Silverbeck
Jumps Road
Churt
Farnham
GU10 2HL

Tel. +44 (0)1252 795951
Fax +44(0)1252 790777

Email: enquiries@carbolicsmokeball.com
Website: www.carbolicsmokeball.com

First published in Great Britain in 2007 by Carbolic Smoke Ball Co.
Copyright © CSBC Ltd

The right of Jan Davies to be identified as the author has been asserted in
accordance with the Copyright, Design and Patents Act 1988.

ISBN 978-0-9556557-0-8

British Library Cataloguing in Publication Data
A CIP record for this book can be obtained from the British Library.

Printed by the MPG Books Group in the UK

for Christie

About the author

Jan Davies has been engaged in criminal advocacy for over 20 years. From 2001-2007 she was a senior crown prosecutor at CPS Abingdon. She currently practises in both magistrates and crown courts, mainly for members of Reading Solicitors Chambers, of which she was a founder member.

Contents

1.

Starting Out

Advocacy is like lion taming. There are numerous books on how to do it, but there is no substitute for going in among the lions. Every day someone gets eaten. Every day some unfortunate solicitor or barrister is berated by a judge in court and made to look small. The normal courtesies which should be expected from persons in authority towards the vulnerable are not always observed. There is little preparation possible for the experience of being denigrated in public. You will learn the craft on your feet and not from any book. So what follows is only a suggestion as to how to survive. Just as the tamer needs to find his or her own unique way of communicating with the lions, so you will need to develop your own unique style and your own survival techniques. There is a limit to what any book can do for you.

Is the profession for you?

Firstly, looking stupid goes with the job. If you think of yourself and the impression you make only in terms of your image rather than in relation to how you can prosecute a case effectively or do the best for your client, then you are doomed to failure. The basic principle is that he who would save his life shall lose it. If, in order to keep your sanity, you need the good opinion of other people, then give up now. The Bar or the solicitors' profession is not for you.

If, however, you wish to persevere in criminal advocacy, perhaps with the hope of doing something for the public or for the wrongfully accused, then you may come to enjoy being part of a great profession and the sensation of fellowship with your colleagues. You will also enjoy endless opportunities for nosiness. Police officers, if you are prosecuting, will tell you all manner of tales. When you are defending, you can ask a defendant anything about his life and he will tell you. After a while, particularly if you practise in a provincial town, you will know which pubs not to drink in, who is going out with who and will receive more dubious pieces of information such as where is a good venue for finding drugs. If you enjoy studying human nature with all its foibles, then this is the job for you. Despite the increasing interference from the Legal Services Commission (LSC) in your legal aid cases and the flow of edicts from those who seek to introduce criminal procedure rules to rival the complexity of the High Court, it is still a job in which you have some opportunity to exercise your professional judgment. Stick with it!

Dress

For the Crown Court, the dress code is clear: dark suits for men with white shirt, white tabs, gown and (if you are a barrister) a wig, with black suits and white blouse or black dresses for ladies, white collarette and (again only for barristers) a wig. In the world in which I grew up, trousers for ladies would have been unacceptable in any workplace. Once they were allowed in the Royal Enclosure at Ascot, however, they became acceptable almost everywhere, provided they are part of a suit.

- *Ladies*
  In relation to what has been called the Great Hosiery Debate, you may get away with having no tights in the summer if you are wearing trousers, but if you are showing

any leg at all, it is best to wear tights. Also, keep your arms covered, at least to the elbow. An exhibition of flesh is not going to be appreciated. I have a black garment purchased in a back street in Tehran which covers almost everything: it is good enough for the ayatollahs so it is good enough for the crown court. You might also be well advised to forget wearing flamboyant makeup. The judge won't like it, others may wonder how it is that you had time to put it all on in the morning and it is unlikely to win you any respect.

- *Gentlemen*
  Avoid the type of stripes in a suit which make you look like a performer on Brighton Pier. You are going to court, not to a male modelling session. You can forget the hair gel too.

Some solicitor advocates are obsessed with not being allowed to wear a barrister's wig. Forget it. The convention is to change in 2008, but the jury, if they think about it at all, may feel you look more human than your opponent. On no account suggest to your opponent that he apply to take his wig off! If you have an advantage with the jury, you might as well keep it. You may well encounter prejudice from members of the Bar if you are doing your own advocacy, of which more later. It is all best ignored, like an attack of the hiccoughs.

For the magistrates court the dress code is more relaxed but it is still expected that you will dress soberly – suits for men rather than sports jackets and formal day clothes for ladies. I tend to look like a Greek widow most of the time – I feel safer that way – apart from perhaps more soft coloured clothes for the youth court.

You will notice that I will be always referring to the defendant as 'he'. I am assuming that those reading this are far too sensible not to realize that 'he' also includes the possibility of the defendant being 'she' and appreciate that to keep mentioning this would make for tedious reading. I am not one of those who believe that the Bible should be rewritten so that 'mankind' becomes 'humankind' or some other non-word.

Similarly, many advocates nowadays are female. Gone are the days when I would walk into a court like Tower Bridge magistrates and find I was the only woman solicitor there. (I used to pick up quite a bit of work in such places. People would come up to me and start telling me their life stories thinking I was from probation or social services and then when they realized their mistake would want me to represent them.)

When you begin

The first time I went to court to represent someone I had only been in a magistrates court once before. I had spent most of what were then known as articles (traineeship) sitting behind counsel in the crown court. There was no money for my employers in sending me to observe the magistrates court. On the morning I was admitted as a solicitor, I was sent to a court in east London. "Go over there and get an adjournment," I was told. I arrived to find that the case had been adjourned twice already. The prosecutor considerately let me look at his file (I had no papers) and told me the case was listed for committal. It was clear even to me from the five pages of prosecution evidence that I had no basis for asking for another adjournment, but although I knew what committal was, I had absolutely no idea what was involved in the court hearing.

I began by sitting on the bench reserved for juvenile defendants. The police officer running the court politely told me to move. When asked I managed to say yes, I agreed that the case should be committed. That wasn't too difficult. "Have you any applications?" asked the stipendiary magistrate. Applications? What sort of applications? My bewilderment must have been obvious. "Well, wouldn't your client like her bail to continue?.... What about some legal aid for the crown court?.... What about the witnesses?" Well, what about the witnesses? I had no idea what was being asked of me. "Don't you think they might need to come to the hearing?"

I crawled out of court feeling six inches tall. It was, however, a salutary experience. Thereafter I always turned up at court very early and watched what other people were doing – when to get up, when to sit down, what worked and what didn't. The first rule of survival when you are starting out is turn up early, watch what others are doing, observe everything closely.

The witness service take witnesses into court before the start of the list so that they can observe the layout and who sits where. If you are in a court you have not visited before, you should do the same. In the crown court the defence advocate sits closest to the jury. In the magistrates courts the defence advocate is closest to the dock, if the dock is at the side of the court, and the prosecutor is closest to the witness box. If in doubt, ask someone, an usher perhaps.

Each court has its little ways. In some magistrates courts the court clerk will decide which case is heard next based on information put onto a slip of paper by the advocate or hoarsely whispered across the court room. In others it is the usher that you need to cultivate as he is the person with the power to ensure that your case is called promptly or that you are kept waiting at court until late afternoon. Do not lie to any of these people. You may get called on first by saying that you will "only be two minutes" but if the case then takes twenty minutes to deal with, they will remember you and the next time when you really are going to be quick, no one will believe you. Honesty will pay off in the long run.

The next rule of survival is to show respect for the magistrates, district judge or, if you are in the crown court, the judge. You may not like the look of them but you are stuck with them. They may not, incidentally, like the look of you either. But normal good manners are for people we perhaps wish we did not have to speak to: only ever get angry with your friends. You will find this the best way to preserve your sanity.

Showing respect is not always easy. You will be subjected to criticism that at times will seem unfair and you will have no means of answering back. Here is a list of some of the things you *cannot* say:

> "The solicitor instructing me is a complete twerp and I have no idea what this case is about."

> "Someone else put together this bundle of papers. I would never have decided to prosecute this rubbish."

> "My client is completely mad. He won't listen to anything I tell him. If you think you can do any better with this idiot then help yourself!"

> "Yes, I know this defence sounds daft. I think it's daft too. What do you expect me to do about it?"

> "You want a defence statement? You must be joking. I can't make any sense of this case whatsoever. It's a complete cat's breakfast."

> "Help!!"

Do not swan into a small local magistrates court assuming that you are the only one who truly understands what is happening. Your slightly dusty chairman may, for all you know, be a professor of law. He may well have sat on the Bench for more years than you have been in practice. The wily old buzzard will not be impressed by a display of petulance. He has seen it all before. Remember, too, that if you are counsel in the magistrates courts you start with ten minus points. The Bench may expect you to waste their time by repeating yourself, they may expect you to be condescending and arrogant. Some of your colleagues before you may have soured the atmosphere by forgetting that they are not in front of a jury (though whether juries appreciate repetitive cross-examinations is another matter). There are, of course, ignorant magistrates just as there are bullying judges, but your task is to deal with your own case, not to show off your legal expertise. I once had the misfortune of co-defending with a young counsel who demanded to know the "reasons behind the reasons" why bail had been refused and said that "in all my years of experience I have met nothing like this". He looked as if he was barely out of short trousers: almost everyone in the courtroom must have had more experience than he had, including his client.

So be aware of who is hearing your case. In a court where you appear frequently, you will soon find out about the disposition of your magistrates or judges. There was one particular stipendiary magistrate (district judge he would now be called) when I was practising in London who was known for his attempts to scarify young advocates. (I am not, of course, going to tell you which court this was, and I appeared in courts all over London so it is pointless for anyone to try to guess!)

Many times I felt like throwing down my notebook and walking out in disgust. He had the uncanny knack of knowing when I was almost at breaking point and would then make some disarming remark, such as telling a client of mine "I was going to send you to prison but your solicitor has persuaded me otherwise. She has influenced me greatly." It was almost as if he knew precisely when exchanges might go too far. I learned a great deal in his court and probably would not otherwise still be in practice.

One point of etiquette

In the magistrates court the Chairman of the Bench will usually say good morning to those in court at the start of a session, and may wish you good morning personally at the start of your case. It is courteous to reply. Say good morning to a crown court judge, however, and you are in trouble. It is simply not done. The judge may wish everyone good morning if hearing an application in chambers behind closed doors, but never in open court.

First hearings

I am concentrating on the magistrates court because that is where you will almost certainly begin.

If you are prosecuting, you should have read the papers in advance of the first hearing. If you haven't and the Defence decide to enter a guilty plea at the first hearing, you may well be ambushed and find yourself hastily cobbling together an account of what happened from an inadequate case summary. It may not be easy to find time in a busy office for preparation of a court the next day but you need to insist on it. Do not let yourself be chivvied into doing courts 'blind'. Quite apart from your professional obligation to be prepared before you go into court, you never know what the future holds. Some day you may want to join the independent Bar or even defend or join the court service. It will do you no good to have a reputation for sloppiness, and since you are going to have to do this court list, you might as well do it properly.

Your first problem when defending may be legal aid. As I write, the Legal Services Commission are in the throes of messing up the legal aid scheme irretrievably. For many years the courts have been served by a patchwork of solicitors' firms across the country. The government decided it did not like small suppliers, but experiments in setting up public defender's offices failed. They were found to be expensive and did not attract clients. Of the eight offices that started in 2001, four are closing. Anecdotal evidence suggests that they could not attract sufficiently dynamic staff and that their operation was hobbled by bureaucracy. So now the plan is to introduce competitive tendering in 2008 and deliberately to put some firms out of business. Small firms will not be able to compete. There is a threat that a threshold of an annual turnover of £50,000 is to be introduced, thereby putting many sole practitioners on the scrap heap, irrespective of whether they have been giving good service to their clients. Don't ask me how this is supposed to fit in with support for small businesses.

I could write a great deal about this subject, but it is beyond the scope of your survival guide. The only point I would make in relation to your first hearing is that if you are defending you must be sure you are going to be paid for what you do. The labourer is worthy of his hire – or so it says in the Bible – and if you take on a criminal case you will indeed be labouring.

Once you have appeared for a client in court, the court will expect you to be there on subsequent occasions and your reputation may suffer if you are not. So make sure you submit a legal aid application if your client is a person of slender means *and* do not promise to do any further work unless and until it is granted.

Many of us remember the old legal aid forms with their questionnaire about means and requirements for 13 weeks' wage slips. (Since many people before the criminal courts work in the black economy and have no evidence of employment whatsoever, this caused problems, with dubious letters on headed paper to try to confirm income. I even wrote "occupation – burglar" on one form accompanied by "I have no legal source of income" and supplied the charge sheet as evidence.) There were so many difficulties trying to assess the incomes of people living on the edge of or outside respectable society that the means test was scrapped and a collective sigh of relief went up in magistrates courts' offices all round the country. Now, means questionnaires have made a comeback, but the system is even more draconian than it used to be because there is no mechanism for someone to pay contributions if they are of modest means but working: legal aid is either granted or it isn't, and if it is not, then there is no help at all to be had unless you are prepared to do the case for what will almost certainly be a pittance and send your client a bill which he very probably will not pay.

So do not promise to do anything, other than perhaps to apply for an adjournment, without a legal aid certificate in your pocket or at least the firm promise of one. The court clerk may bark at you, but the blame lies with those who decided to introduce this hurdle. Previously, the court clerk would have been able to make an assessment on the spot. Now the application has to go to some administrative person in the court office, who has no knowledge of the case, has not heard what the prosecution says about it and most importantly has not seen how inadequate the defendant is to deal with the allegation himself. If you are barked at, remember it is not your fault. Stand your ground and point this out.

Your next step, having made sure that someone will pay for your services, is to see what you can find out about the prosecution case. The standard of what is known as 'advance disclosure' depends on which CPS area you are in. Ideally, you should have a copy charge sheet, a case summary, statements of the main prosecution witnesses and a record of your client's interview. You may find that there is no transcript of what was said at this stage, but that the gist of the interview is contained in the case summary or perhaps in a statement from the interviewing officer. It is always open to you to get a copy of the tape of the interview. Your client has an absolute right to this, and if you are appearing outside your usual area, ask the prosecutor at which police station the Tapes Clerk can be found so that you can write and ask for it, or ask your instructing solicitor to request it. The tape will usually come from the police, not the Prosecution. Your client is also a source of information.

If he is able to give you sensible details about his case, he should know what he said to the police. However, what he tells you may not be accurate. Years ago one client of mine told me that he had confessed all to the police, even though he was innocent, because he had been refused a cigarette, was desperate for a smoke and had been promised a packet once he had told the police what they wanted to hear. I got the tape of interview and listened to it. The police station concerned had recently been declared a no smoking zone. Smoking was not even allowed in interview rooms although members of the local CID who were also desperate for the comfort of nicotine regularly smoked in interviews, secretly, without the permission of their inspector and in fear of detection. Cigarette butts were removed from the waste bins at the end of an interview. When I listened to the tape, I could hear what sounded suspiciously like the striking of matches and then my client saying "ah, that's better", and what might well have been a reflective pause as he took a sustained puff. Later in the interview I could hear an exchange of words which made it clear that he had accidentally set fire to some papers in the waste bin with the stub of his cigarette. The interview itself sounded quite relaxed. The flap by the police officers about the smoking bin appeared in the transcript as "We spoke of other matters". To his credit, once I told my client that I had listened to the tape, he did look somewhat sheepish and stopped complaining about the interview.

Now that you have got the papers from the prosecution read them – all of them. This may sound like elementary advice, but do not assume that the case summary will be accurate or that it will tell you everything.

Particularly in confusing cases of affray or group disorder the case summary may not be much help. The police officers may have been quite clear as to what they did, but muddled about what happened before they arrived. It is also possible that the case summary may have been written before all the main statements were written, that prosecution witnesses contradict themselves. A common problem is trying to identify who did what. Defendants described as 'Male 1' and 'Male 2' by one witness may be described as 'Male 2' and 'Male 1' by another. The descriptions of what they were wearing or of their physical appearance may well be contradictory. This may or may not be significant. Witnesses remember different things about an incident or will have been observing at different times. It is up to you to try to piece together the jigsaw. If you are prosecuting, you may find it helpful if the police give you a description of what each person was wearing on arrest and a basic physical description.

Similar problems can arise with drugs cases. The police do a raid. They find various quantities of drugs in different parts of the house. It is perhaps multi-occupied so the first question is who lives in which room and, if there are admissions, precisely what has each defendant admitted.

A shoplifting case often depends on video evidence. It can be a reflex action to ask for the CCTV. Ask yourself first whether you really need it. If your client is *compos mentis*, tells you he was stealing and confessed to the police once he got caught, the video is not going to help him and he will not get the maximum credit on his sentence from the Bench for entering an early guilty plea. Also, the prosecutor may well tell you that you are not entitled to it in the circumstances as you have quite sufficient information on which to advise your client and the court will simply label you as a time waster, which will do your client no good. On the other hand, the CCTV may well be the only evidence in the case, and your client may tell you that he or she was not there. I once persuaded the Prosecution to drop a case because when I watched the video I could see that the person stealing could not possibly have been my client: the hair of the person concerned was far too tidy. My watching the CCTV – I knew what he looked like, whereas the prosecutor did not – undoubtedly saved the court the time that would have been spent on a pointless trial.

So when defending get to court early enough to talk to the prosecutor and to find out what you can; similarly, if you are prosecuting, do not waltz in just before 10 o'clock. Useful conversations happen early in the morning. The Defence may well have something of interest to tell you, and arriving early will ensure that you have laid out your files (I used to find strict alphabetical order a help) and are ready for whatever is thrown at you. If the front door of the court is closed until shortly before the court starts, find out where the back door is and insist on using it.

Some people, once they have moved into what they see as prestige serious crime, forget about the court below and assume that nothing interesting happens there. The magistrates court is, however, the place where many important decisions are taken and the place where the prosecution and defence lawyers meet for the first time. Nowadays a Crown Prosecution Service lawyer is involved at the police station stage in all but the most trivial of cases or in cases where it is obvious there will be a guilty plea. The decision to charge should therefore have been a carefully considered one and the chance of your changing it by blustering at the Prosecution lawyer at the first hearing will nowadays be small. However, the decision will have been taken with no input from the Defence. Prosecutions should not just be brought because the police can prove what happened: they have also to satisfy the somewhat nebulous concept of 'the public interest'. The Code for Crown Prosecutors can be found on the Crown Prosecution Service public website. It will not necessarily help you to understand what the 'public interest' means, but essentially one question to be asked is "is there any point in prosecuting?" or "even if convicted, what would any court do with this person?". Thus, for example, someone who is learning disabled or mentally impaired (or whatever label is suitable in the circumstances) may well be aware of what he has done, may know in some way that he should not have done it but have a level of responsibility for his actions which is not very large. There may be no point in punishment for such a person. Or you could, to take another example, be dealing with what is known as a 'domestic' incident, in which one spouse or partner has pushed the other, any injury was trivial and although the police were called and the perpetrator spent the night in the cells, they have turned up at court together arm in arm and a prosecution would quite simply be a waste of time.

Such questions are usually not capable of resolution at the first hearing. To take the two examples I have given, if you are prosecuting you will need something more than the defence solicitor telling you in a hushed whisper that his client is mad before you will drop a case on mental impairment grounds. You are going to need something more convincing and it is up to the Defence to supply it. Similarly, you are going to need more than the defence advocate telling you "she has said she wants him back" before you drop the domestic assault case. What seems trivial may be part of a disturbing pattern of aggressive behaviour and it may be the umpteenth time the police have been called to that address. It is also even possible that what you are being told is quite simply wrong and the lady sitting with her arms entwined round the defendant in the court foyer is not his wife. You need an adjournment and to send the officer in the case an urgent request for some further information. Nothing, unfortunately, can be taken on trust, although the Defence solicitor is doubtless telling you what his client says in good faith.

So it is more than likely that you will need an adjournment of the case. Here are some examples of how this can be requested:

"There are some urgent inquiries I need to make of the police."

There is not enough evidence on this file. I want the officer in the case to get some – soon!

"I will be asking for this case to be reviewed."

This prosecution really ought to be dropped but I need authorization. If I am pushed into talking to a manager on the phone this morning, I will almost certainly be told to continue with it. Give me a week and I'll try to get it discontinued.

"My client needs to take some decisions about his case. It would be very helpful if I could have a short adjournment so that he can consider his position fully."

I have tried. He won't see sense. But if you give me some time to get him into my office without his wife/girlfriend/obstreperous aunt I just might – no promises mind you! – get him to do the sensible thing and plead guilty.

> "I need to get the tape of his interview and listen to it."
>
> *He says the summary done by the police is useless. If I am able to listen to the actual tape myself I shall know whether we have a time-waster or a genuine not guilty plea.*

When you have got the adjournment make sure that you use the time wisely. If you are prosecuting you need to send the police a memo by whatever is the speediest route for your local area, by FAX or email. If you are defending and you need to speak to your client in your office before the next hearing, try to make an appointment for him before he leaves court and give him a note in his hand. You do not want to turn up for the next hearing having done nothing.

2.

Bail Applications

Many defence advocates begin an application by saying "My client has a right to bail…" and go on to cite the presumption in favour of bail from the Bail Act, but there are few types of hearing for which the law matters less. The court will find a more practical approach more helpful than references to cases and statutes. The questions to be asked are what is the risk of letting this person out, either to the general public or to the individual witnesses, is he likely to do it again while he is on bail and then questions about where he is going to live and whether there are any conditions that will keep him under wraps while the case is going through the courts.

The issue of bail often arises at a point in the case where the defence advocate knows more about what is going on than the prosecutor. He may have sat through lengthy interviews in the police station the night before, he may have represented the defendant on numerous occasions previously so he knows far more about him than can just be gleaned from a list of convictions and he may also know the defendant's family. As a prosecutor, you may just find a file of papers dumped on your bench at court when you arrive in the morning, or if you are unlucky, the papers will not arrive until the middle of the morning, long after everyone has been asking you whether you are opposing bail or not and numerous other questions about the case. If this happens to you, insist on some time to read your file and to decide on whether you are applying for a remand in custody and, if so, why.

Deciding on bail is one of the most important tasks you have. Depriving someone of his liberty before he has been found guilty is a very serious matter indeed. Just because the police don't like his father, or dislike his attitude in interview, that does not mean he has to be locked away. If you can, speak to the officer in the case. Use the telephone – start collecting direct dial numbers for your local CID, robbery teams and other useful persons if you have not already done this – although in a serious case, you might expect an officer to have taken the trouble to come to court personally to speak to you. Five minutes with someone involved in the investigation can completely change how you look at the case, either in favour of bail or against it. But do not let yourself be intimidated. If you are not as experienced as some of your colleagues, some police officers may realize this.

Busy police officers are not necessarily going to have the time to hang around the court until the case is called – you would hope they were back out arresting villains – and it will be appreciated if you take the trouble to ask the officer for his mobile number or police station extension and let him know what happens to the application if you do decide to apply for a remand in custody. Feedback of this nature is always useful for the police.

Get as much information as you can. If you are told that "he has two cases pending" ask where and what stage they have reached. If they are cases at a court in your area, the court computer should be able to provide answers, or if you have your own prosecutors' room in the court building with a computer, you should be able to look on your own system and find out what is going on with this defendant. It can be embarrassing if you are told by the Defence in open court that a case you said was pending has in fact been discontinued for lack of evidence. Similarly, if you are told that the address that is being suggested is "unsuitable"* you will want to know why. It can be embarrassing, for example, if you tell the magistrates that there is a "risk of interference with witnesses because his address is close to that of the victim" and then discover that the two addresses are ten miles apart and the defendant cannot drive. It is better, if you can, to ask questions before you start, rather than in the middle of the application itself.

Work on the principle that those who might hurt each other should be separated. The Defence may well tell you that there is no risk of the defendant doing anything so unwise as to go round to the home of the person he has assaulted. Do not take any chances: put a condition onto his bail, if bail is going to be granted, that he should not go there, preferably that he does not enter the same part of town at all.

There are different ways in which remands in custody are sought. One person against whom I could never get bail when I was defending was a fragile looking lady in Thames Valley with a mind like a rapier. Under the guise of being an old English rose, she would put all the points for a remand in custody so gently yet so thoroughly that you could see the Bench thinking "well, if *she* says we should not let him out, we really should not risk it". Conversely, I can remember another prosecutor who always sounded so aggressive that my applications seemed often to attract sympathy.

You will need to find your own unique style when applying for remands in custody, but I would recommend only asking

---

*'Unsuitable' can be shorthand for a nest of villains/drug addicts or a squat.

for remands when you truly believe it to be necessary. If you think that bail, if granted despite your objections, should be conditional, then you should outline the conditions you want at the start – unless you are very sure indeed that bail will be refused. Residence, reporting to the police, curfew between certain hours and no contact with named witnesses are the usual options. I was very much in favour of curfews for burglars, not just as prevention but as a constant reminder of their wickedness, though this is not a reason that appears in the Bail Act. Young men – and burglars are usually young men – do not like having to be at home in the evenings.

When you are defending, if you have not met your client before, the list of his previous convictions is a good place to start. The magistrates, if they retire to think about whether to grant bail or not, will take the list with them. Examine it closely. Does it suggest to you that he offends when he is on bail? You may find that on a previous case, when he was sentenced he had a large number of offences, and it may be obvious that they were not all committed at the same time and that therefore one or more of the offences was committed while he was on bail for the rest. Ask him about it.

Also ask him about his address, who lives there, how long has he been there, and whether he is the legal tenant. If he is living with his girlfriend and she has the rent book (a common situation for reasons not unconnected with the DSS), is she prepared to have him back?

There are particular problems with 'domestic' cases of assaults on girlfriends or cohabitees. (You will notice that I do not use the word 'partner'. There are still some members of the Bench or judges who do not altogether care for the term. I tend to refer to someone as 'his young lady' or 'the person he lives with'. It makes me sound old fashioned but my client will almost certainly be calling her 'my girlfriend' or 'my Mrs.' and I am not in the business of sounding like a social worker.) You may need to be thinking of an alternative address, at least while the case is pending, and you may well run into the problem that your client obstinately refuses to consider alternatives, telling you that "I know she wants me back". You may even find his girlfriend sitting in the court foyer anxious for a word with you and desperate to have him home. Speaking to her is a minefield, as you really should not discuss the case with her and especially not her evidence. There is, strictly speaking, no property in a witness, but you do not want to find yourself accused at a later stage of having persuaded her not to give evidence. You could suggest to the prosecutor that he has a word with her instead, but may well find that the prosecutor does not think it appropriate at this stage either, on the basis that she is perhaps not the person she says she is. In the past I have dealt with this situation by asking another defence solicitor to have a word with her, totally independent from me, so that at least she can have some support from somebody. But this, of course, depends on finding another solicitor prepared to help. However distressed she seems, it may well be that there is nothing you can do. The defendant will probably in any event have to go and live at his mother's, his sister's or on a friend's sofa.

Think practically. If he was arrested the night before, he will have not so much as a toothbrush with him. How is he going to get his clothes and washbag? He needs a contact in the police station who can arrange a time when an officer can go with him to collect the things he needs, or permission for a neutral third party to retrieve them. Mention this to the court.

It will help no one if he goes straight round to her flat after he is released, to collect his clothes, and is re-arrested for breaching his bail conditions.

Also, when you are sorting out an address – or indeed anything else – be very careful not to lie to the court. People in the cells are desperate to get out. They will tell you "My mum will definitely let me stay there". When you ask him for a telephone number for his mother and phone her up, she may say she will not have him back at any price and give you an earful about what a pest he has been recently. You then have to make a doleful second visit to the cells to speak to your client again. If you then say to the court "my client tells me that he can go to his mother's address" without telling the magistrates the true state of affairs and she then complains to the police when he turns up on her doorstep, you could then be in serious trouble, suspected of perverting the course of justice if you are unlucky and at best acquiring a reputation of being devious. Your ideal situation is being able to say to the Bench "He tells me he can stay at his mother's. She is sitting at the back of court. Perhaps you would like to have a word with her." That way you are covered. If there is no inquiry you can make, then something like "My client tells me he can go to this address" keeps you out of trouble.

Rarely, in these days of livescan checks in the main police stations, you may have a problem with his identity. Years ago, when I was just starting out in the courts, I was telephoned by one of the jailers responsible for the cells of one of the central London courts and told that a Mr. Smiggs (not the name I was really given of course) was in custody and asking for me.

"I don't know any Smiggs," I said.

"He's asking for you personally," I was told.

Not wishing to turn away work I went over to the court and visited the cell block.

"You are not Smiggs," I told the client. "I remember you. You're Bloggs. I represented you last week."

"No, no, I am Smiggs."

Now, I would simply put my coat back on, grab my bag and leave the court building, briefly pausing to tell the jailer that I could not represent him. Then I was unsure how to deal with the situation. I went into court and spoke to the police officer who said he was dealing with the case of Smiggs. "Have you any list of convictions in the name of Smiggs?" I asked.

The list contained a conviction for rape and various convictions over a long period of years for indecent assaults. I went back to the cells.

"Are you sure you are Smiggs?" I said, posting my copy of the list through the hole in the cell door.

"The bastard!" shrieked the client. "No, no, I'm Bloggs. He told me he was clean. Tell them I'm Bloggs. I *want* to be Bloggs."

It then emerged that he had bought a medical card from someone in a pub who had told him he could use it as proof of identity if he was ever arrested.

Providence was looking after me that day. You cannot be too careful. If you *know* that your client is not who he says he is, then leave him to his own devices and do not represent him. You are in very serious trouble indeed if you mislead the court, even by your silence, when he gives a false name to the clerk.

You will find that people will promise anything in order to get out of custody. They will tell you that they are prepared to 'sign on' at the police station every day, stay at home every night from 6 p.m. onwards and never go to the place where they might meet the complainant. However once bail is granted, they will start to whinge about having to keep to the conditions and you will be asked to make fatuous applications to vary them. A common ploy is for him to say that he is going to start working night shifts or at some distance from his home and that he will find it impossible to report to the police daily or to keep to his curfew. Explain to him that the courts have heard all of this before numerous times and that he needs a letter from his future employer to show the court if he wants to apply to vary his bail. Very possibly you will hear no more about the promised job.

Most of the people you represent will not know anyone suitable to be a surety. In order to be a surety, a person needs not only to be able to satisfy the court that he/she has the means to promise to pay the court a fixed sum of money if the defendant does not turn up at court but also must be a person of 'good character'. Firstly, your client may have no one in his family who could perform such a function, and secondly, if they are respectable people and if he has been in trouble on numerous previous occasions, they may not wish to take the risk. Parents can surprise you. One mother who had expressed concern in numerous telephone calls while her son was in custody at the police station over a weekend, when asked if she would consider being a surety said "Certainly not. It's time he learned a lesson. He ought to be put away for a while." So do not suggest to the Bench that a surety is an option unless you are sure that you can produce a suitable person. There is no point in having bail with a condition that cannot be fulfilled.

Applications in the Crown Court

If bail is refused by the magistrates and your client wants to appeal, then you will need to draft a written application to the crown court, send it to the list office, perhaps telephoning first, depending on what your local court likes best, to check when they can list it for hearing. Bail applications at this stage are in chambers, with no need for a gown, unless you are dealing with a case that has been 'sent' (of which more later). It is best to put full details into your written application. Otherwise you run the risk that the judge will read it before you address him and will have already made up his mind on the basis of the very little information on the form. There is a standard form for the application. You will need to attach the certificate that the magistrates have heard a 'full argument' if you are making the application pre-committal and a list of the defendant's convictions.

Crown court applications can be very speedy affairs. The defendant is not normally present. I can still remember the days when you could ask for your client to be produced for the bail application. Then everyone seemed to decide that this was just too much bother and applications were dealt with in the defendant's absence. Personally, I think this is unfortunate. A defendant really should be present when his liberty is being discussed. Without him the whole business can become far too cosy, with the defence advocate starting off by saying something like "I realize there are difficulties in the way of this application", which can be tantamount to saying "Look Judge, I know this is hopeless, so do you, and I'm just going through the motions". On the other hand, at least you know, sometimes before you start, as you do not with a lay Bench, precisely the height of the gate you are trying to get over. One judge (now, alas, deceased) used to say when looking at a particularly long list of previous convictions "I presume you are making this application on instructions." "All my applications are made on instructions" I would reply virtuously. "Yes, but some more than others. Well, you had better get on with it…" I knew before I started that the application could not succeed. Similarly, when I was applying for bail for a man who had robbed a bank using a gun, I was told "It's your duty to apply for bail, I suppose. I shall hear you with interest and no enthusiasm."

You have to face the fact that some applications, however spirited, are not going to succeed, and indeed that some ought not to succeed. Very experienced defendants may even tell you they do not want bail. They want to notch up some time on remand to count against their sentences, thereby serving time in custody with the benefits of being as yet unconvicted and entitled to regular visits.

You will no doubt find your own way of communicating with clients. You are going to be asked frequently "What are my chances?" Never promise a person that he will get bail unless you are completely sure that the application is bound to succeed. You will find life easier if your clients get nice surprises rather than disappointments, and they will learn to trust you too.

3.

Plea Before Venue

In 'summary only matters' (cases which can only be tried by magistrates) the procedure for dealing with pleas is simple: the defendant either pleads guilty or not guilty. He should be able to understand what is happening without difficulty.

Cases that are indictable only and have to be heard at the crown court whatever the circumstances, like murder, rape or kidnapping to mention only a few, are 'sent' to the crown court instantly without the magistrates having to know anything about them. Some crown courts still have what are known as preliminary hearings as their judges will have decided (sensibly in my view) that the sooner they take control of a case the better. Others will list their first hearings many weeks away, which seems to remove any point to sending the case there so speedily as everyone involved then has a snooze for several weeks, including the defendant who may avoid all contact with his solicitor if he decides to be an ostrich. So far he has not had to take any decisions about his case at all. No one has asked him what his intentions are.

The cases where there is a serious decision to be made are those which are either way, – which, if the defendant pleads not guilty, can be heard either in the magistrates court or in the crown court depending on a) which venue the magistrates think is more suitable and b) if he is given a choice, where the defendant would like his case to be tried.

Decision time

The clerk begins by reading out a long involved announcement.

As you may have been asleep when you last listened to one of these, forgive me if I quote from the Magistrates Courts Act 1980, Section 17A. (The section was inserted and then amended by recent legislation. You can find it in its entirety in Archbold.) First the charge, which has to be written down, has to be read to the defendant. "...The court shall then explain to the accused in ordinary language that he may *indicate* whether (if the offence were to proceed to trial) he would plead guilty or not guilty". He has to be told that if he *indicates* a plea of guilty "...he may be committed for sentence to the Crown Court..." and that if he *indicates* a plea of guilty then the court will treat him as if he had pleaded guilty.

I am always amazed that defendants behave as if they understood this gobbledegook. First it says that the court will treat him as if he had pleaded guilty, and then the section of the Act goes on to say that asking him whether he would plead guilty or not guilty if the case proceeded to trial "shall not for any purpose be taken to constitute the taking of a plea".

So an *indication* of a plea of guilty is not an actual plea, but the court will treat it as if it were. An indication of not guilty in the magistrates court thus does not count in the crown court and he can decide when the indictment is read to him there to plead guilty after all. But the judge will probably find out about the previous indication anyway. You may wonder, as the defendant stands bemused in the dock of the magistrates court convinced that what he is doing is entering a plea, who drafted this nonsense. Some courts have simply given up, and just give the defendant a handy paraphrase rather than using the words of the statute.

The court clerk will also tell him that he would get a discount for a guilty plea (only he won't say what that will be of course as no one knows what the sentence would be, so it is not much of an incentive) and the defendant who has by now probably become totally confused is told that he should not plead guilty unless he is guilty (because we don't do plea bargains in this country, do we).

Let us assume that a defendant has indicated a not guilty plea. The next step is for the Bench to decide whether they will keep the case or decide it is too serious for them and it should go to the crown court. At present the magistrates' maximum power of sentencing on an either way charge is limited to six months' imprisonment. The Criminal Justice Act 2003 increased their powers to twelve months, but this is not yet in force as I write, and if and when it does come into force, it is going to have a big impact on the number of cases which stay in the lower courts. No one yet knows what the effect is likely to be.

So, contrary to what many defendants think – that it is their choice whether or not 'to go to Crown' – the first decision is one for the Bench: will they agree 'to keep it down' or 'send it upstairs'?

Prosecuting

At present, we are all still dealing with the six months' maximum, so the question for the prosecutor is "would this person get more than six months?". If you are prosecuting for the Crown Prosecution Service (CPS) you will have had full details of your charging standards and mode of trial guidelines and should know what are the aggravating features which push a case towards the crown court. You will also find a very helpful section in Archbold. (*Archbold: Criminal Pleading, Evidence and Practice,* revised annually, a most useful and unfortunately expensive tome). There should also be in your file the detailed note of a prosecutor who gave the pre-charge advice in the police station which ought to include an opinion about where the case should be tried. This document is on no account to be disclosed to the defence. It is a privileged exchange between the CPS and the police, often with some opinions expressed robustly. If you are an agent, make sure you do not give the defence a copy by mistake.

Remember that the decision is made by the Bench, not by you, and that they only need sufficient information to deal with the decision on venue. You are not opening a case before trial or giving full facts before a sentence. They only need to know enough of what the case is about to decide how serious it is. If they have a busy court list to get through, they will not thank you for a long-winded presentation. However, you should not sound as if you are just painting by numbers. You need to make sure they know enough about this individual case to make an informed decision. For example, if it is a drugs case, they need to know the quantity involved, the street value and the circumstances in which it was seized. If the defendant was arrested inside a night club with numerous wraps of heroin which he was likely to sell, then tell them about it. If an assault in the street involved a particularly vulnerable person, such as a young child or a disabled person, then they need to know. (You may, however, wish to exercise a little caution before referring to a victim or witness as 'elderly'. My own guideline is to use the word only for someone over the age of 70, and 'retired person' in other appropriate circumstances. People, including magistrates, are active well into their late 60s these days or longer.) For a theft, they need to know the value of what was taken: most shopliftings are dealt with in the magistrates court, but theft from an employer, particularly where there have been numerous thefts and the defendant had some system, can be viewed seriously.

Some cases, however, are so serious that you will need to give very little by way of facts. I am particularly thinking of sexual assaults on children or of serious child neglect. You may find that you do need to say very much about some of these.

In a complex case you would hope to have looked up some sentencing cases in advance, but beware of citing the court of appeal too enthusiastically. Most appeal cases are appeals by the defence against a sentence deemed too severe. The appeal court is considering whether a particular sentence is unjust, not necessarily what is usually the most appropriate sentence in all such cases. The magistrates may anyway have dealt with a case similar to yours before and have a very good idea of what they themselves would do on sentence.

Lastly, do not be overly distressed if you point the magistrates in one direction and they decide to go in another. It is not your problem. If you have argued for summary trial and they have sent the case to the crown court instead, then when you reach the crown court and the judge asks why is this case here and says that he doesn't see why he should have to deal with it, you can tell him that it was the magistrates' decision and not the fault of the prosecution. So mark your file carefully with the result of the hearing and do not lose any sleep over your disappointment.

Defending

How do you approach the decision on plea and venue if you are defending?

The short answer is with caution and make sure that the

defendant understands at every stage what is going on. The decision whether to plead guilty or not guilty may be the most difficult one he will make. If the magistrates decide that they could hear the case, then he will be asked where he would like his case to be tried. Here he will also need your help. Should he go for a jury, with possibly a better chance of acquittal but with possibly heavier penalties if he is found guilty?

One factor in his decision at present may be legal aid. If he is working then he may not be eligible in the magistrates court for any assistance. In the crown court there is at present no means test. If his case is complex and you may need to obtain an expert's report or if there are numerous defence witnesses to interview, it would be foolish to pretend that he is not going to be influenced by the legal aid position. Costs in the magistrates court can be a real problem. There are plans for the Legal Services Commission (LSC) to take over the granting of legal aid in the Crown Court and introduce a means test there too. Most crown court judges do not like dealing with unrepresented defendants and are not going to like having people in front of them with no counsel or solicitor. Most judges are barristers and have been insulated against having to deal with people direct. If the Legal Services Commission are wise they will quietly forget the idea of introducing means tests in serious cases. It only needs one case of obvious injustice for the court in Strasbourg to become involved.

Some likely communication problems

A friend of mine who was working years ago as an immigration adviser had various initials that he used to put on the front of his files so that anyone taking a file out of his cabinet would know instantly the type of advice that had been given. There were various options: G.H.Q. stood for 'Go Home Quick', G.O.K. for 'God only knows' when a person's problem seemed incomprehensible, T.T.F.O. for 'Told to F**k off' and F.O.L.E. for 'Facts of Life Explained'. I rather like F.O.L.E. You should be able to put it on all your files or endorse it on all your briefs. You do your client no favours at all if you do not explain to him the position he is in honestly and realistically. Sadly, before he tries to convince you that when he was emerging from a window at dead of night with a bag full of someone else's silverware he was actually practising for some work as Santa Claus, he will have already convinced himself. Some people have an infinite capacity for self-deception. "It ought not to have happened" becomes "it didn't happen", and the self-deception can become entrenched to the point where he believes it himself.

Here are some lines you may be able to use:

"It's not me you will have to convince..."

"Some people might find this difficult to believe."

"You will be in the witness box, not me."

"I wouldn't want you to have a trial and then just end up in a worse mess."

But do not 'lean' on the person. There is a fine line between robust explanation and 'leaning'. It is not your case, it is his.

Friends and well-meaning relatives will ask you "how can you represent a person you know is guilty?" But you don't actually *know* anything. You were not there when the incident happened. You are not judge, jury or magistrate. What no one ever asks you is "what does it feel like to represent someone you believe to be innocent when you know that he is going to be convicted". There is a rape case which I prepared when I was doing my articles which still haunts me. I became convinced that the guilty verdict was wrong. Mercifully you may find there are not many such cases but unless you are completely hard nosed you will find these distressing. So do at least listen to your clients when they tell you about what happened. Make sure they understand that you can only advise them according to what they tell you and that they know what their options are. Not all of them will have already made up their minds what to do before they go into court.

One factor in the decision to choose a crown court trial can be the complexity of a case. If there are going to be issues of inadmissibility or arguments about disclosure of unused prosecution material, it is often better to have a judge in control, rather than magistrates having to perform a near impossible balancing act of hearing about evidence and then deciding to take no notice of it. Another factor may be the timescale involved. Contrary to what many believe, not all your clients want to prolong matters interminably. Some of them may prefer the certainty of a fixed trial date which the magistrates court can give them, although given the clog in listing these days with the shortage of clerks and the insistence of some courts on having pre-trial reviews before anyone will even think of setting a trial date, you may even be better off in the crown court if speed is what your client wants.

Committals

Once it has been decided that the case should go to the crown court, then apart from the cases that are 'sent' it will be adjourned for committal and the Prosecution will be wanting an adjournment (four weeks if the defendant is in custody and usually six weeks otherwise) to prepare their bundle of statements. The Prosecution should serve their bundle in advance but you may find it is given to the Defence on the morning of the committal hearing. Very often if you have had copies of statements at an early stage you will be able to deal with committal on the day the papers are served. Provided the bundle shows a *prima facie* case (my test is if you were on a jury would you think the defendant had some explaining to do at the very least), then there may be no point in delaying. You might as well tell the court clerk the case can be committed.

Another future development will be the abolition of committal proceedings where the magistrates decline jurisdiction and they say that a case has to go to the crown court: such cases will then be 'sent', with the same procedure as for indictable only serious cases. Crown court judges who may have been unaware of the amount of work that goes on before committals will then have to deal with the chaos. The advantage of a committal hearing, if you are defending, is that you can punt your client, who has been carefully avoiding you for weeks, into a side room, confront him with all the prosecution statements and then ask him what he has to say about them. It is also an opportunity for the prosecutor to bark at the police. If the papers are not in good shape for a committal hearing, then the Prosecution may decide to ask for the case to be discharged.

Mentally disordered offenders

There are numerous people you will meet in the criminal courts who are thought not to be in need of treatment in hospital but who are described as "having a personality disorder". I was once told by a psychiatrist that my client had a personality disorder. He then said, "I suppose you're going to ask me what that means... I think what I am trying to say is that he's weird." This was not helpful, but at least he was more honest than most.

Such people drift in and out of hostels which do not want them, end up in lonely bedsits with so-called community care which seems to consist of an occasional visit from a social worker, they self-harm and have problems with alcohol and/or drugs. As things are at present, there is almost nothing you can do for them, though at least for the duration of their case there will be people rushing around professing an interest, although not any intention of helping. If you manage to get such a person voluntarily admitted into a hospital, you will find he is discharged after a short time, even without any inquiry having been made into where he is going to live. The probation service won't want him. Probation these days consists mainly of managing people in discussion groups. If a person will not fit into a group, he is said to be unsuitable for probation supervision. There is very little of the intensive one-to-one work that used to be done. The excuse is made that there are no resources to deal with such a mentally disorderd person and that he would not understand the requirements of a Community Order. You may ask what is the point of prosecution at all in the circumstances: it should be a matter for social services.

But the difficulty you will have if you are prosecuting is that this may not be the first time he is in trouble and in the absence of a hospital place with a compulsory Mental Health Act order you are stuck with having no alternative but to prosecute. If, for example, he has attacked one of his neighbours yet again, or gone around the street ripping wing mirrors off cars and punched someone on the nose, doing nothing about it is not an option. Also, you cannot just drop a case without some *evidence* of mental disturbance.

Typically what happens is that the case is adjourned for medical reports, perhaps even a report into fitness to plead. He does not co-operate and won't keep appointments with the doctor. Eventually he ends up in prison because that is the only solution for making sure the report is done and for dealing with his constant breaches of bail. Then he will have served the equivalent of a six month sentence and unless someone is able to come up with a hospital place, he will end up being released only for the whole miserable cycle to begin again. Until we as a society devise some way of coping with such people there is often almost nothing constructive that any court can do.

You may possibly be better off in the crown court with such a person, and the Bench may agree. A judge has more powers than magistrates – although magistrates can make hospital orders too. It is beyond the scope of this little Guide to go into too much detail, but have a look at the Mental Health Act 1983 if you have not already done so, specifically Sections 2 and 3 which deal with compulsory admission to mental hospital outside criminal proceedings, and Section 37 (hospital and guardianship orders made by the courts) and Section 40 (Home Office transfer from prison).

The Earl of Shaftesbury (the one who campaigned for chimney sweeps) believed that morality was linked to efficient drains and also that ordinary people were just as able as doctors to decide when a person was mad. I would recommend a sort of mental checklist when deciding whether what you need is an assessment of fitness to plead:

- Does he know who he is?
- Does he know what he is said to have done?
- Is he able to tell you whether he did it or not?
- Does he understand that whatever it was is wrong/illegal?

If the answer to any of these is no, then you might start thinking about raising the issue of fitness to plead, which these days in the crown court is decided by a judge, and organizing a medical report, for which you will need funding from the LSC. (Again, you will find the procedure in Archbold. Almost everything you need is in Archbold and you will find everyone else in the crown court is using this useful volume too.)

Some ethics

Occasionally you may be asked to run a 'bent defence'. Don't go there! There are good professional rules for how you deal with such a situation and they are there for your protection. If you *suspect* your client is not telling you the truth, you do not have a professional problem – because you are not judge or jury and just because you don't think his defence is credible that does not mean you should deprive him of the right to be heard. You may want to give him robust advice in his own interest, but it is the court which has the final decision about whether he is to be believed.

But if he tells you he is guilty but intends to go into the witness box and say something different and especially if he is going to call witnesses to say what he knows to be untrue or misleading, then you need to withdraw the hem of your garment – fast. People have to be able to talk to their lawyers in confidence, but unless he speedily sees the error of his ways, you will need to tell the court that you cannot act for this defendant. The expression 'professionally embarrassed' will suffice: without giving details, you will need to ask to withdraw from the case altogether.

The most common situation you may encounter is a proposed false alibi. Years ago a person accused of a serious crime confessed that he was guilty but then said to me "But that's all right. My girlfriend will come to court and say I couldn't have done it because I was with her."

No, I said, it was not all right, I didn't run cases in this way, and did he really want his girlfriend to run the risk of being prosecuted for perjury?

"Well, my previous solicitor thinks nothing of doing this sort of thing," he retorted.

"I don't think so," I said. "I know your previous solicitor rather well."

"Don't see how you could," grumbled the defendant. "He's in Liverpool."

"I've got news for you," I said. "He's my brother."

At least he had the good grace to look sheepish and to accept that what he wanted me to do was just not going to happen. What my brother said when I told him this tale is not printable.

Similarly, you may be in the position of having a list of convictions produced that you know is incomplete or even hear the prosecutor tell the court that your client is a person is of good character when you know this to be untrue. The Police National Computer is by no means infallible and the records produced can have mistakes. On no account indicate in any way that you are confirming an incomplete list as a truthful one. You may even think it prudent, if asked to confirm that the list is accepted, to point out that it is the Prosecution's job to check the list.

You need to preserve your reputation. Behaving honestly and being seen to behave honestly will be important not just for the cases you are currently dealing with but for all those cases in the future when the court needs to know that you are trustworthy, and if you have acquired a reputation for sharp practice, that will affect how the court views your future clients.

4.

Preparing for Trial in the Crown Court

A trial is a trial, and it can be just as frightening conducting a trial in front of an acerbic district judge in the magistrates court as it is in the crown court where everyone has to maintain a certain level of courtesy because there is a jury present. A trial with a district judge is going to be faster, and probably with more adverse comments as you struggle through. Some district judges seem to regard it as their mission to scarify young advocates.

Just as counsel start with ten minus points in the magistrates court, so if you are a solicitor you may encounter some prejudice from callow young persons who should know better in the crown court. It is not so long ago that barristers were trying to keep solicitor advocates out of some robing rooms. "We have to put up with you lot cluttering up our rooms in the magistrates courts," I remember hearing one solicitor telling some sniffy counsel. There is a great deal of foolishness still around, although you will find that the criticism is muted because you are, besides being competition for the cases you may be doing yourself, also a potential source of work.

Many years ago when I was working for the film director Stanley Kubrick and had been upset by the rudeness of a certain actor, he told me "Don't worry, actors are not people." Sometimes you may feel that this could be said of some members of the Bar. But I have also met with great courtesy and benefited from useful advice from many barristers, and I trust, if you are a solicitor, that you will too.

The first time I was in the crown court I was representing a burglar. He was subject to a crown court suspended sentence and knew, as I did not, that if he pleaded guilty in the magistrates court and was committed for sentence then he could ask me to represent him rather than "having to have some barrister". I was by no means sure he was right, but when I looked at the rules it was clear that if the solicitor had represented the defendant in the court below, then on a committal for sentence he had rights of audience in the crown court.

I did not want to be there. I was only there because my client insisted. The case started with the judge mistaking me for an usher. However, once we had cleared that up and established that I did have the right to be there we got on with the business in hand.

Nowadays solicitors are not an uncommon sight in the crown court. CPS lawyers are starting to conduct many of the hearings themselves, and prosecuting in the magistrates courts is being left to designated case workers, or DCWs, who are people trained by the CPS but who have no legal qualification. The changes are doubtless all being pushed through for no other reason than to save money and insisted upon by people who have little understanding what can happen in a busy magistrates court and no appreciation of how serious the consequences can be of the cases that are heard there. We are now in a society in which a thief can get away with a fixed penalty of £80 for shoplifting of goods up to £300 in value and a person who puts out her rubbish on the wrong day is fined £300. Whether we like it or not we have moved into a world in which crime to some people, and I don't mean the victims, does not matter.

So the future for many advocates is likely to be in the crown court. Work in the magistrates court may dwindle. Solicitors will just have to get used to it – penguin outfits and all!

Crown Court Plea and Case Management Hearings (PCMHs)

A PCMH used to be a fairly simple affair, with the plea entered and the case adjourned for trial or for a pre-sentence report to be prepared. At my local crown court there used to be a one-page form for the advocates to complete, which gave an idea of the length of the case, which witnesses were required and any particular problems. There might be individual difficulties that were mentioned orally to the judge. Then some committee (one suspects containing some civil lawyers and certainly a number of bureaucrats) designed a 10-page form. It only has space for one defendant on it so if there are a number of defendants each defence advocate must produce his own form, unless someone has managed to download a multi-defendant form from the internet in advance. The front of the form declares "This form is to be used at all Crown Court Centres without local variation". Any practices which a particular local court have found effective in the past have to be jettisoned.

Anyway, if you are defending, you had better fill it up and then give it to the prosecutor to fill in his bits before it is handed to the judge. The court should provide you with a copy of the completed form after the hearing. The important section is the list of witness requirements. If you are prosecuting, do not assume that if the defence decide they do not want a witness to attend then you will necessarily not want him at the trial either. There can be good tactical reasons for wanting live evidence and good tactical reasons for the Defence saying they do not want him.

There are also forms for Bad Character applications. Letting in a person's previous convictions is a relatively new procedure, so I have added a short appendix to this book on page 80, which is brief but I hope useful. There are forms for Hearsay applications, and again I have produced a very short appendix on page 83. There are forms for Special Measures applications, where arrangements are sought for witnesses to give their evidence screened from the defendant or by live television link from a separate room. Nothing, it seems, can be done without a form. It is almost as if those who introduced all this paperwork would have liked the trial to be conducted by post. Why the more simple Special Measures applications, for example, for very young witnesses where the application is automatically granted, cannot be dealt with orally is not explained.

Scrutinise every piece of paper that is thrown at you and make sure that if there is anything you want to say about it, you either say it at once or ask the judge for permission to raise an objection within a suitable time limit. If, for example, there is a Special Measures application for a video to be played as evidence in chief, make sure that you have had the opportunity of watching it to check whether there are any portions that are inadmissible. No one is going to be pleased if last minute editing of video tape is required a few days before a trial – and this problem can arise just as easily if you are prosecuting and have neither seen the video nor obtained a transcript.

And then there is the Defence Statement. Ideally this should have been served on the court and the Prosecution in advance of the hearing, but in reality statements are often handed up to the judge at the PCMH, often because the defendant has been an ostrich about the whole case and has not kept appointments with his solicitor. The requirements for what a Defence Statement should contain are set out in the Criminal Procedure and Investigations Act (known as the CPIA) 1996, sections 6A-6E and like everything else of any substance you will find this in Archbold.

Some of these sub-sections are not yet in force. I predict that if it is decided to bring into force section 6E which says that the Defence should serve a notice giving the names, addresses and dates of birth of defence witnesses, it is going to be difficult for many defence solicitors to comply. Persuading defence witnesses to come to court at all is often very hard indeed, without giving them the additional worry that if the police know they are going to give evidence, they may start bothering them by stopping them in the street for no good reason. There are likely to be very few notices, even though such fears may have little foundation in many cases. We are likely to find dates of birth and names disclosed hastily on the day of trial, and in this computer age the police will then be able to check whether the witness has a criminal record in a matter of a few minutes. It is not likely that a witness is going to agree to his address being disclosed in advance, and though many lawyers are not keen on quoting Human Rights law, it would not be right to disclose addresses and dates of birth without permission. We can also anticipate arguments about 'equality of arms' because there is a strong convention that if you are defending you do not contact prosecution witnesses and certainly the police are not going to give you their addresses.

We shall see. In the meantime, if you find yourself drafting a Defence Statement at the door of the court – for which incidentally as counsel you will not get a separate payment – then make sure that the client understands what is being given to the court in his name. Too often a Defence Statement looks like something that is more suited to the High Court and has come off a word processor. Some judges do not like brief statements, but the statement is only required to set out 'the nature of the accused's defence' and 'matters of fact on which he takes issue with the prosecution', why the defendant 'takes issue' and whether there are any points of law 'which he wishes to take and any authority on which he intends to rely for that purpose'. Since the Statement is supposed to be the statement of the defendant not that of the solicitor this last requirement seems unrealistic, but you need to do your best to ensure that the defendant understands what is happening. There are special rules for alibi defences: witnesses to an alibi should be disclosed, which was the situation under the old law.

The Defence Statement may trigger some disclosure in addition to the Schedule of Unused Material and copies of any items the Prosecution think should be given at this stage, although if your client has answered questions in the police station then the nature of his defence should already have been obvious from the content of his interview and anything potentially useful should have been sent to you already anyway. The old maxim of 'When in doubt say nowt' no longer applies in police interviews if you want to avoid criticism at trial, and if your client has answered every conceivable question put to him by the police you might want to put into his Defence Statement somewhere that he tried to tell them the truth.

Trying to draft the Defence Statement at the door of the

court may not be realistic with some defendants, but you can hardly tell the judge that your client's attitude is useless. You have to indicate obliquely what the problem is and hope that the judge picks up your frantic signals. Here are some signals you can send, together with what you may be thinking but cannot say:

"I am having some difficulties in taking instructions this morning. It might assist if my client could have the benefit of the advice of the solicitor who has the conduct of this matter. Would your Honour grant 14 days for the statement to be served?"

I cannot get any sense out of this person, but his solicitor has looked after his cases for years and can be trusted to hit him over the head with her umbrella. She is not here this morning, having better things to do than to hang around this place!

"There appear to be some mental health issues."

He's mad. I can't cope with him.

"I am not sure that my client fully understands the position. We have a statement in draft but it has not been signed."

He won't listen to me. I have waved a perfectly good statement under his nose which reproduces what he said in the police station and he just won't read it. He doesn't see why he should. If Your Honour could just explain to him why it's needed, perhaps he will listen to you. I don't seem to be getting anywhere.

"I appreciate that the statement is somewhat brief."

Quite frankly, the Prosecution are lucky to be getting any sort of statement – and there's nothing to say anyway. It's all in his interview. If the prosecutor would only read the record of interview for once instead of constantly carping ....

Then having waded through all these formalities, you are at last told when your case is likely to be listed for trial and you can all scuttle out of court. In the crown court it is considered very bad manners indeed to leave the judge on his own in the courtroom with no counsel present, so wait until he either 'rises' (goes out for a cup of coffee) or another brace of advocates arrives for the next case.

5.

Trials

*"If you can meet with triumph and disaster,
and treat those two impostors just the same..."*

Rudyard Kipling

Any gathering of criminal lawyers, whether at some summer party or in one of the crowded pubs round Chancery Lane, can become seriously boring. They all seem to be talking about themselves. Some of them are not so much talking as braying. "...so then I said this...and the judge said that... and I looked at the jury...". But you will soon discover that there is nothing so invigorating as a good win, walking out of court with that special feeling of triumph, and you need to share it instantly with colleagues who will understand the skill you think you have just displayed – and that there is nothing so disappointing as feeling at the start of a case that it is one which you cannot lose, only to find the case fall apart. You have to tell someone about it, preferably another lawyer.

However the truth is that some cases deserve to be lost: either because if you are prosecuting your witnesses turn out to be disreputable and the Bench can see through them, or if you are defending, because your client really is guilty and it becomes obvious. Very little of what happens when you lose may be your fault, and equally sometimes you should take little credit if you win. You simply cannot tell how a trial will turn out until you see the witnesses in the witness box. What appears straightforward on paper may turn out to be quite different.

So if you are defending and looking at the case the night before – and yes, I know you should have prepared it all weeks in advance, but the reality if you work in a disorganized place is that the file or brief may be thrown at you with little notice – do not despair. I shall never forget going to court to defend an assault case. On paper it looked bad: the use of a weapon was alleged by the 'victim' and a photograph showed an injury which seemed to prove it. The chief prosecution witness turned out to be a hefty gentleman with an aggressive manner. My client was a little shrimp by comparison. My first question in cross-examination (and I have no idea why I asked it) was "After he hit you, did you say anything?" "Yeah," came the instant retort. "I told him he's dead!" At this point it seemed that the Bench lost interest in the prosecution case. Maybe they decided that they did not care whether there had been a weapon or not. I don't know, but the behaviour of the 'victim' in court came as a surprise to both me and the prosecutor. It was not predictable on the face of the papers.

Pre-trial preparation

If you go on advocacy training courses, you will be told that you should have a case plan, you should have your tactics worked out in advance. It may be suggested that you should 'brainstorm' the case, writing down every piece of information that you can think of about it, a somewhat similar method to some meditation techniques. You may be encouraged to think in detail about your cross-examination and any speech you are going to make and to write everything down.

There is nothing wrong with any of this provided you do not then get stuck to it to the extent that you cannot depart from your plan without hesitation or anxiety. If you stop listening to the witnesses because you think you know what they are going to say, then you are likely to be ambushed.

What is important is that you should have everything that you need. There is no point in going in to bat with no pads. If you are prosecuting, check that you have your statements arranged in the order you expect to call your witnesses, check you have your Section 9 statements (the ones you are going to read), a record of the defendant's interview and that the Defence have agreed that you can read the Section 9 evidence, check that any exhibits you will need to produce to the court will be available. In an ideal world these checks should already have been done for you – the world is not ideal, so check yourself as well. It also makes sense, particularly where you have a number of charges, to go through the witness statements matching what is said to the individual charges and reminding yourself of who proves what.

At least when you are prosecuting you do not have to hare around trying to find witnesses, because the police witness care unit will do it for you and will arrange for a police officer to find someone if it is necessary. I once, when defending, went into five different pubs in Reading one evening, leaving messages all over the place about a hearing the following morning. No one had mobile phones in those days, except for police officers and drug dealers, because they were too expensive. The pub visits worked: the following day I found the witness sitting at court waiting for me. Magistrates courts trials are not such a problem because at least there is a fixed date for the hearing, but some crown court trials are listed with notice only being given late the afternoon before, although you should at least be aware that it is likely to be listed some day during a particular fortnight.

People will constantly surprise you. Those who you think will definitely turn up on time seem to have problems even getting out of bed, while people who constantly fail to keep appointments and seem to be going around like chipmunks on speed will turn up for their trials looking quite spruce and on time.

Years ago a bomb went off at our local railway station and the whole town centre was closed. My client usually came to court by train and he was always late, sometimes not turning up at all but telephoning the court with a series of flimsy excuses. So on the morning of the aftermath of the bomb I did not expect to see him at all and was quite surprised to find him waiting for me at court looking most annoyed because I was wandering into the court building shortly before 10 o'clock.

"Where have you been?" he demanded, "I have been here since 9.30."

"I didn't think you would be able to get here," I said.

"Well, I'm not going to let those bastards stop me from coming," he replied stoutly. "Of course I'm here, and *you* are late!"

Trials – order of play

There is a set framework for all trials: prosecution opening, prosecution evidence, defence evidence, defence closing speech, with the Prosecution also making a closing speech in the crown court before the defence advocate has the final word with his closing speech. Once you get started you are likely to be so absorbed with what you are doing that you will forget any nerves, and in any event nervousness, remember, is not the same as panic.

Imagine that you are in front of a lay Bench in the magistrates court. Opening the prosecution case can be more difficult than you expect. Do not rely on the police case summary unless you are sure that it is accurate. It may be full of police-speak. Officers do not get out of cars, for example: they 'alight' or even worse, 'exit'. They 'proceed' rather than walk. If you find yourself reading out this type of language because you have not taken the trouble to think about how you will present your case, all you will do is succeed in giving the Bench a good laugh.

You have to say enough to tell them what the case is about, but not go into such detail that they then have too great an expectation of what the witnesses are going to tell them. A victim of an assault, for example, may give the order in which events happened somewhat differently from what he told the police in his statement. The basic facts will be the same, he has no doubt about who struck him and what his injuries were, but months after the event his recollection does not completely match the account he gave shortly afterwards when he was lying somewhat dazed in hospital. On the other hand, in the magistrates court this is your only chance to speak to the Bench yourself about the case. Explain what it is you have to prove and what evidence is available to prove it.

Before you start, when the witnesses arrive, and are shepherded by the usher into some side room so they can wait without having to bump into the defendant and his cronies, you should have been out to speak to them. This can be difficult because as professional rules are at present you should not discuss their evidence with them. You should only hand them the originals of their statements to the police so that they can look at them to refresh their memories, maybe explain briefly what happens in court and then leave them for the witness support volunteer or the usher to look after.

So unless the police have told you, you may have no idea of the quality of the witnesses you are going to call. Just having no previous convictions does not make a person respectable. You will undoubtedly have some surprises, both good and bad ones. The demure young lady who claims she was attacked in a nightclub turns into an aggressive harpy in the witness box, while the police officer who you previously thought was a lazy waste of space turns out to be your star witness.

When you are defending, you have at least talked to your client. You know only too well what he is like, and once he goes into the witness box he will forget all the wise advice you gave him about concentrating on the questions he is being asked, about not answering one question with another and not getting sarcastic with the prosecutor. There is nothing you can do for him once he goes into the witness box. He is beyond your help, and if the case is adjourned for lunch while he is in the middle of giving his evidence, you should ask the Bench to explain to him before they rise that you cannot speak to him over the luncheon adjournment: you will have to eat your sandwiches somewhere else. You should have explained to him beforehand that when you are 'examining in chief' you have to ask him questions about what happened without suggesting to him what the answers will be. He may well preface some of his answers with "as I told you last week…" or "you know what happened next". Ignore these slips like an attack of the hiccoughs and press on. Make sure that he tells the Bench his side of the story.

If you are calling witnesses to back up your client, remember that they may not have had the benefit of being asked to recall the event shortly after it happened. Obtaining legal aid can take time, and the defendant will have had no solicitor to help him until after he was charged, often months after the offence is said to have been committed. So the details may not match, although the gist of what they are saying is essentially the same.

In a closing speech, after calling witnesses who had disagreed with each other on points of detail, I once observed that the accounts of the Resurrection in the Gospels differed greatly from each other, in that one Gospel had two angels, another had one, but that this was often taken as proof that the witnesses, while they remembered it all somewhat differently, had not got together to concoct a story.

"Ah," said the chairman of the Bench wisely, "but you have not exactly got angels as witnesses, have you."

You may have learned that you should not ask a question in cross-examination to which you do not know the answer. But when you cross-examine you are asking questions on the basis of what your client has told you, and some questions have to be asked. Remember that you cannot start giving evidence yourself when you make your closing speech. If you want to suggest an alternative version of events to that given by prosecution witnesses, you need to have put this alternative to them in cross-examination.

There are basically two types of witnesses: the ones you challenge and the ones you try to make friends with. Some witnesses will be people who are not involved in the incident in any way – the woman who says she was being nosy peering through her net curtains at what was going on in the street, the passing motorist who stopped and called the police on his mobile phone to report what looked like a fight out of control. Such people do not deserve to be harangued when they are in the witness box, and you will not get the sympathy of the Bench or a jury by badgering them. Try what charm can do instead.

When I was doing my articles all those years ago, I spent many hours sitting behind counsel in the crown court. The best closing speeches were short, directed to the jury with plenty of eye contact, not given from notes and were intended to create the illusion for the jury that they actually witnessed the event themselves. A good advocate seeks to make the magistrates or jury feel that they know and like the defendant, with all his human weaknesses, and that they do not *want* to convict him.

As for the verdict, I quickly gave up making predictions because I was always wrong. In one particular case (for reasons I cannot obviously explain) I had a very strong belief that my client was innocent. The judge summed up briefly and sent the jury out early in the morning. They did not come back until late in the afternoon, by which time my client, who was in the cells, and his girlfriend were both frantic with anxiety. I was not feeling any too good myself. Eventually they came back with a verdict of not guilty, and my client and his family collapsed into sobs and smiles outside the court. A lady on the jury came up to my client's girlfriend and said "We just want you to know. We none of us at any point thought he could have been guilty." What, I wanted to ask, have you been doing then for the past four and a half hours? During the evidence, this particular member of the jury had looked most disapproving. If anyone would have decided on a guilty verdict, I would have thought it would have been her. Verdicts continue to surprise me.

Domestic cases

A special word about 'domestics' because these can present particular problems.

It is fashionable to talk about 'victims' of domestic violence. A person is not necessarily a victim until the court decides that she is. I am using the word 'she' in this context, because although there are some men who suffer from domestic violence, it is more usually the woman who is treated by the police as the aggrieved party. Officers attending a house after a 999 call and confronted by two people who have had a fight will usually arrest the man. If I am defending I refer to her as the 'complainant', because although we may not know who is telling the truth about what happened, we do know she is complaining. Not everyone wants to be called a victim anyway. It could be thought insulting. Some prosecutors will stick to calling her 'the aggrieved'.

The difficulty with such cases is that they so often involve one person's word against another's with very flimsy corroborative evidence – some reddening on a person's arm, a broken vase, an overturned chair. Then she comes to court and says she does not want to give evidence, or simply stays away despite having been served with a witness summons. The fear must be that if she is forced to give evidence against her will then the next time she is assaulted, she will not ring the police and the result may be injuries that are far more serious. On the other hand, if someone makes a complaint to police which results in another person being arrested, spending many hours in a police cell and then being subject to bail conditions obliging him to leave his home and causing total disruption to his life, then that person should see it through and not just decide not to come to court. There are some difficult decisions here for prosecutors, and whatever you do, you may wish you had done something else.

Trials have their own momentum. Witnesses are called and have to be asked questions. They can be far less scary than prosecuting a busy remand court with a large number of files and an irascible Bench or being court duty solicitor the morning after St. Patrick's Night. Read your case thoroughly in advance and you will survive!

6.

Sentencing

"We have been over-legislated to. Acts amending and altering, declaring and explaining, prohibiting and encouraging, enacting and repealing heap our Statute book with provisions creating the evils it would remedy. Every fresh meddling increases our helplessness and we pray to be let alone."

William Hone, 1817

If this were a textbook this would be the longest chapter. Sentencing has become more and more complicated and if I were to write a detailed précis for you of the sentencing principles to be applied in every case, it would be out of date within six months. This government has introduced constant changes and even the judges are having problems in keeping up. The Attorney-General has now issued an instruction that prosecutors: in 'complex cases' or where there is scope for 'misunderstanding' (no definition as to what this means) should set out in writing the aggravating factors for sentencing and the judge's legal powers. As it is, a crown court judge will often ask the prosecutor "What are my powers?" and if you are prosecuting, you must know the answer. You should also know the answer if you are defending, because if by mistake an illegal sentence is passed you too have an obligation to point out the error.

In the crown court, start with Archbold, and make sure it is an up-to-date version. You may have a problem if the offence with which the defendant is charged is a 'historical' one because only the current law appears in Archbold. The defendant has to be sentenced on the basis of the charge he faces, not on the basis of what would have happened if he had committed the offence at the time he is being sentenced. So, for example, if he is charged with an offence under the Sexual Offences Act 1956 he has to be sentenced in accordance with the penalty prescribed in that Act, and not as if it were an offence under the Sexual Offences Act 2003 (which incidentally did not come into force until April 2004 just to confuse matters further). You cannot ask the judge therefore to make a Sexual Offences Prevention Order, which you might have been able to do if he had been charged with a 2003 Act offence.

This is just one example. It is all horrendously complicated, and not helped by Acts coming into force piecemeal, and even Archbold will not always help you. For example, Section 25 of the Identity Cards Act 2006, which deals with the possession and production of false passports, driving licences and various other documents, came into force before it had found a place in the 2006 Archbold.

In such circumstances, you may have to resort to the internet to look at the actual wording of the statute concerned. Statutes passed in 1972 and from 1988 onwards can be found at www.opsi.gov.uk/acts.htm. This can be a valuable place to start in many situations rather than wading through official guidance and emails. Look for the maximum penalty and make a note for yourself of what it is. Do not assume if you are in the magistrates court that the offence is imprisonable and carries six months. Some offences carry less than the six months' maximum. Criminal Damage, for example, carries a maximum of three months. Many, like Section 5 of the Public

Order Act 1986, do not carry imprisonment at all. If you are in the magistrates court the court clerk will usually be the person to advise the Bench, but you need to be alert too. Expecting the court clerk to know everything is not a safe attitude.

Having found out what the maximum sentence is, then you might want to start looking at some case law. Courts are now obliged to pay some attention to the Sentencing Guidelines Council. You will find a useful compendium of court of appeal judgments on their website, www.sentencing-guidelines.gov.uk. Again, Archbold may also be a useful source of information, though the magistrates courts tend to be more familiar with Blackstone's and you may also find the court clerk referring to Stone's Justices' Manual. (Personally, I have never found Stone's very useful: the index can be puzzling.)

Trying to assess the seriousness of your individual case is likely to be your next step. You may find a reported case with facts that are 'on all fours' with your own, but otherwise you will be looking for 'aggravating' and 'mitigating' factors. Sometimes there will be a leading case that will spell out for you what these may be. Very clear guidelines, for example, are set out for the sentencing of burglars in <u>McInerney</u> (2003) and for the sentencing of those who are caught with child pornography in their computers in the case of <u>Oliver, Hartrey and Baldwin</u> (2002). Some people will tell you that you should set out everything fully for the judge or magistrates, but if you know that they have sentenced more burglars than you have ever prosecuted or represented, then you need to strike a balance between appearing to deliver a totally superfluous lecture and making sure that the relevance of the facts is appreciated. If you have all the facts and legal principles in your head, you will be equipped to be sensitive to the reactions of the Bench or judge and to appreciate when you need to shorten what you had planned to say. It is always easier to truncate than to expand an address.

Never try to look as if you know the answer to a judge's question if you do not. A court will forgive ignorance, but never dishonesty.

Bear in mind too that the judge is not the only person in the court room. Members of the public are there too, and sometimes members of the victim's family. Where, for example, there has been a serious accident caused by a piece of dangerous driving and a passenger has been badly injured, the judge may want you to spell out for the benefit of others in court that his powers are limited to two years and that he has to give a discount for a guilty plea. You will probably get some sort of signal from him that he wants the legal position set out in full.

If you need to write out a version of the facts for yourself, then this may very well be useful. I find dates and times of incidents difficult to remember, and no one is going to expect you to remember details of cheques in a large fraud so having them in large type at your elbow can be essential. But try, so far as you can, only to bury your head in your notes when you really need to, and stay off the jargon.

Road traffic cases

A special word about road traffic: it can be far more complicated than expected, and because it does not usually attract the benefit of a legal aid certificate many of us do not bother to familiarise ourselves with the principles of the minor offences. Then, just as you think you have successfully negotiated the minefields of sentencing for a theft or a nasty assault, the court clerk produces a batch of papers which have surfaced courtesy of the court computer and consist of various summonses for using a vehicle without insurance, driving 'otherwise than in accordance with a licence' or even failing to stop after an accident which is imprisonable. You can, if you like, say it is all nothing to do with you and scuttle out of court leaving your client to sort it out by himself, but he won't thank you for leaving him and the court will wonder why, when you are there anyway, you are being so unhelpful. You are not going to be ambushed like that in the crown court because offences like No Insurance will be listed on a schedule prepared in advance, but you may well find that the judge is unfamiliar with minor road traffic matters and is going to need assistance.

So if road traffic offences are involved, check whether there have to be penalty points endorsed on the defendant's licence, whether the Bench must disqualify and if so, for how long. If you are defending, remind your client he must bring his driving licence with him, and check whether there are any points on it.

If he is being sentenced for an offence under Section 12 of the Theft Act 1968 (taking a car without the consent of the owner or driving it knowing it to be stolen) then the sentencing court has the power, though not the obligation, to disqualify him. The aggravated version of this offence, set out in Section 12A of the Theft Act carries obligatory disqualification. It is only too easy for the defendant to be so focussed on whether or not he is going to prison that he completely misses the announcement of a disqualification. In the magistrates court they will sensibly frisk him of his licence before he leaves the court building so that he does not forget and will insist that he signs a piece of paper confirming that he knows he is disqualified.

Some road traffic offences are 'strict liability' offences. It does not matter what was in the defendant's head at the time or what he may have intended: either he has valid insurance or he hasn't, either he has a valid driving licence or he hasn't. However, there may be 'special reasons' why the Bench do not have to endorse his licence. In these days of speed cameras when people are understandably nervous about acquiring points on their licences no endorsement should be accepted lightly. Special Reasons for not endorsing a licence have to relate to the offence itself and not to mitigation. It is of no interest that the defendant is poor – that is personal mitigation – but if he has been misled by his insurance company into thinking that he was insured when he was not, or if he can show that he had good grounds for believing that the car he was driving was insured by its owner for any driver to drive, then if what he says is believed, the Bench may find there were Special Reasons and not endorse his licence. Normally the Bench will want to hear some sworn evidence. Letters from insurance companies are quite often shown to the Bench as evidence of what the defendant believed.

Where personal mitigation applies is in 'totting up' cases where the defendant, by reason of the offence, is going to have 12 points on his licence, and has to be disqualified from driving unless he can show what is known as 'exceptional hardship' which he would suffer if he were to be disqualified.

There is very little case law on this: it is a matter totally within the discretion of the magistrates and although the prosecutor may ask the defendant searching questions in the witness box, essentially it is a matter between the defendant and the court. Loss of his job as a result of the disqualification will not usually in itself constitute exceptional hardship, since loss of employment is a very common consequence of being disqualified, but where the defendant is elderly and unlikely to find another job, where he has a specialized skill and jobs in his field are rare and particularly where he has a young family to support and lives in a place without reliable public transport, the Bench may well decide that they will not disqualify him. Again, evidence is normally given on oath, and often the defendant turns out to be a normally respectable person – which can be a pleasant change in the middle of a busy criminal court list!

Newton hearings

Where there is a wide gap between what the Prosecution say about an offence and what is agreed by the defendant when he pleads guilty, the court may decide that it wants to hold a hearing to try to find out the truth. Such hearings are limited to exploring the area of dissent so not all the prosecution evidence needs to be called. Typically in an assault case, the victim might say he was punched and kicked in a prolonged attack, whereas the defendant might be saying that he only hit him once. Only the witnesses to the actual assault may be required to give evidence. So when the date for the hearing is fixed both Prosecution and Defence need to consider carefully which live witnesses are going to be required.

Remember that the decision to hold a Newton hearing is that of the magistrates or judge. Do not allow yourself to be drawn by a judge or magistrates saying "what are you asking me to do?". You do not know what sentence is being considered or whether the point at issue would make a substantial difference. Sentencing is for the court. This is not America. You can only point out where the main points of difference between the prosecution and defence versions are and perhaps point out also that if there is no hearing, then the defendant will have to be sentenced on his version of what happened, unless it is very obvious that what he says is so ludicrous that it can be disregarded.

In the crown court there will usually be a written 'basis of plea', written by defence counsel or solicitor, shown to the prosecutor and handed to the court. In the magistrates court there is often an unseemly fudge. Both prosecutor and defence advocate will address the Bench, the court clerk may make a note if he is awake and the magistrates may then go out to decide what to do. Particularly if you can see that the defendant is likely to be committed for sentence to the crown court, it would be sensible to write out a written basis of plea, get your client to sign it and hand it in. (Keep a copy. Unfortunately, when the case arrives at the crown court, you may find that it has not reached the crown court file.)

There are two schools of thought about whether, when a case is going to be committed to the crown court, it is the magistrates who should hold a Newton hearing or whether it should be left for the judge. Even in cases where there has been a Newton hearing in the court below, defence advocates may seek to argue that the crown court has 'a duty to inquire' into the circumstances and may ask for a Newton to be held by the judge also. A sensible way out has been that where magistrates decide that even on the defence version of the facts, they would be committing for sentence then there is no point in their trying to hold a Newton hearing, since they will not be the sentencing court anyway. Where the result of a Newton hearing could make the difference between committal for sentence or the case staying with the magistrates, then obviously it makes sense for the lower court to conduct a hearing.

It is sometimes essential for such a hearing to take place. But the victim of a nasty assault, for example, will not be happy when told that although the defendant pleaded guilty, he still has to suffer the ordeal of giving evidence. For cases where there is little divergence between what is alleged and what is admitted Newton hearings are to be avoided.

Mitigation

Your principle task when mitigating is to make sure that the magistrates or judge remember that they are sentencing *this* defendant and that there are consequences for him personally in whatever they decide to do. It may be that there is very little you want to say about the offence itself. Beware of trying to minimise an incident to the point where people in court wonder why your client has pleaded guilty – if you think he did nothing wrong, then maybe you should not have advised him to plead guilty!

Also beware of sounding cavalier about a criminal offence. I once heard a young advocate say to a stipendiary magistrates at Clerkenwell Magistrates Court of an unprovoked attack in the street upon a complete stranger "It was not a very bad assault, sir. He only hit him once." "I will not have such things said in my court," came the thundering reply. If the Bench have the impression that you have already explained to your client the serious situation he is in (and you no doubt have); then they are less likely to be severe.

Look at the police interview. Many people are sorry once they get to court and are waiting for the sentence in the dock. But some are even sorry when they are talking to the police and say so. If you can find an early expression of remorse, then mention it.

Do try to avoid jargon if you can. You may find plenty of jargon in the Probation pre-sentence report. Avoid phrases like "my client knows he has issues to address". What is that supposed to mean? He is unlikely to have thought of "addressing" anything less tangible than envelopes. If you mean that he has a drug problem, it's getting worse and he is at last starting to realize that he has to stop, then do say so. Vagueness rarely helps. It just sounds as if you know you have to say something, rather than that you have something helpful to say. Avoid stock expressions like "a cry for help" if possible.

Most importantly, you need to know about him personally and this requires a personal skill in communication. You will develop your own style with practice. Sometimes I have made a joke of wanting to know about my client's life by saying something like "I am going to sound like a police antecedents' form for the next ten minutes…" (the form police officers sometimes fill up with someone in custody about their background). "I gave her my heart, but she wanted my soul," complained one of my clients, humorously quoting Bob Dylan, although he did eventually understand why I was asking him a string of intrusive questions.

A good place to start could be the list of previous convictions. Where someone has a long list, look for the significant gaps and see if they match with events in his life. You might find, for example, that there were numerous convictions when he was a youngster, then a gap of several years and then it all started again. Was he working during that time? Was he married or living with someone? Was the relapse triggered by any traumatic event, such as a bereavement or a descent into alcohol or drugs?

Or you may find that beginning with his family circumstances is a useful way to begin. "Where are you living at the moment?...How long have you been there?... Where were you before?...When did you last work?..." Work backwards chronologically if he finds this easier. It is like a fishing expedition and you never know what you will find.

Familiarise yourself with the street names and the common effects of different drugs. Your local drugs' counselling service may be able to help you, and may be grateful for your interest. You will then be better equipped to understand what some clients are telling you.

You will need to go through the pre-sentence report to make sure he understands it. Do not assume that he can read. Many people are not able to read anything more complicated than a tabloid newspaper and some are not able to read at all but will be too embarrassed to tell you. So you might want to say something like "Do you mind if I read this through to you slowly, and you must stop me if there is anything you want to say about what the probation officer has written?" Discuss the recommendation with him and find out how he feels about it. If he is truculent and does not want to do any of the unpaid work that is being suggested or keep any future appointments with the probation service, you might need to explain what the alternative might be and to impress on him that he is not at court to receive the Queen's Award for Industry.

Visit the cells afterwards

If your client is given a custodial sentence, then you must visit him afterwards, even when the sentence is an expected one. It is the least you can do. Depending on the circumstances, you may need to advise him on his right to appeal.

I have been constantly surprised by the courtesy with which I am greeted by defendants who have just been sent to prison. They behave much better than many divorce clients I can remember. Occasionally you will be subjected to a hysterical rant blaming you for what has happened to him, only to be sent a letter a few days later from the prison apologizing for his outburst. But whatever his reaction to the sentence, it is he who is going off to prison while you are sloping off back to your office or chambers. He deserves to be treated with dignity.

7.

The Future

The outlook for criminal advocates is grim. Anyone who is in danger of being cheerful when contemplating the future should browse in the Legal Services Commission's website. You will find endless 'initiatives' and 'consultations', meaningless babble about 'taking reforms forward' and making legal aid work 'sustainable', spin expressions to disguise the fact that the service is being cut and standards driven down.

In case you are a member of the Bar or have for some other reason been in happy ignorance in the late 1990s, you should know that criminal legal aid is now limited to firms with a contract with the Legal Services Commission (LSC), the expensively re-packaged Legal Aid Board. Gone are the days when a firm of young practitioners could set up on their local high street and provided they could establish themselves with a reputation for competence, they could expect to flourish. Now a firm needs to jump through the LSC's bureaucratic hoops of franchising before its partners can even consider opening for business.

Consequently there is no new blood coming into criminal work. Last year I attended the Criminal Law Solicitors' Association annual conference in November. This is as large a gathering of criminal hacks as you will find. It was very noticeable that most of the participants either had grey hair or were losing their hair altogether. There are very few youngsters.

Until now the crown court work has been blessedly free from bureaucratic interference. Now the LSC is stretching its tentacles of bureaucracy towards the crown court. On its website is yet another consultation, this time for advocacy assessment. It is to be hoped that the Bar Council is more robust than the Law Society was when franchising of solicitors was proposed, but there are no grounds for optimism. The LSC will start talking about being aware of the need for a 'light touch'. But it will not end there. Those of us who were around back in 1994 when franchising was being introduced can remember Legal Aid Board (as the LSC was then known) officials talking about not wanting to produce 'checklist lawyers'. The pilot schemes were said to be a success, but then everyone always does behave well when there is a pilot. Now all that matters to the LSC is the files, and 'quality' does indeed mean checklists and the ticking of boxes. The LSC dictates when and what solicitors should write to their clients: no one cares whether the client is able to read a letter or whether he wants it – and there are many people with insecure addresses or with curious family members who certainly do not want letters sent to them giving details about why they are in court. The auditing of files for franchising takes no account of individual circumstances.

Similarly we can expect advocacy assessment to begin slowly, perhaps with practitioners being asked to supply references from judges or magistrates, but it will not end there. The time will come when there will be assessors with clipboards at the back of courts or when judges are expected to fill in questionnaires about the advocates' performance. Already judges are going to be expected to tick boxes themselves about the aggravating and mitigating factors in cases they are sentencing, and it is not too hard to predict what is going to happen to all these unnecessary pieces of paper.

Advocacy is not something that can or should be monitored. You have quite enough to worry about with an anxious client in the dock behind you, the judge, district judge or magistrates asking you questions in front of you and your own fear of not doing a good job. Your performance will not be improved by the presence of the person with the clipboard. You should not have to worry about how many boxes that person will be ticking. There are many reasons why you will decide not to pursue what may seem to be an obvious line of argument, many reasons why you decide at a strategic moment that the time has come to sit down and stay sitting down and numerous occasions when you have to say something that your client or the court will not like. You need space to develop your own unique style. You should not be having to justify your every move. To threaten assessment is to compromise your independence. An advocate should be fearless, within the bounds of respect for the court.

But it will be unsurprising if the Bar are lured into co-operating with the LSC because they are too scared to denounce the whole miserable enterprise. Officials in the Law Society appeared too frightened of being seen to be opposing the concept of 'quality' to muster any sustained opposition to exclusive franchising. It may well be that members of the Bar will not perceive where the drive towards advocacy assessment is going. I shall be delighted if events prove me wrong.

The Bill going through Parliament as I write will enable unqualified staff of the CPS to prosecute a wide range of cases in the magistrates courts. CPS lawyers are bound by their professional code of conduct, and *in extremis* can say to their line managers "no, I won't do that, because it's the wrong thing to do". If they are told that they have to have a 'corporate' approach rather than having justice as their main objective, they can refer to their professional code. Unqualified staff are not protected in this way. It is hard to avoid the impression that the change is being forced through not just for reasons of economy, but in order for there to be greater control. Disraeli believed that a country needed strong independent professions: this government appears not to take the same view, and the harassment of lawyers is mirrored by what has happened to dentists, doctors and academics. (This is not a party political point: it was Lord Mackay, a Conservative Lord Chancellor, who first announced that there was to be exclusive franchising of legal aid. We cannot assume that a Conservative government would be any better.)

With unqualified prosecutors conducting more cases in the magistrates courts it is going to be hard to preserve the role of defence solicitors. We are likely to see defence paralegals, often retired police officers, representing defendants. There will be less work in the lower courts for the junior Bar, which is sad as the less serious magistrates court work provides a good training ground. We will see more defence solicitors conducting their own cases in the crown court, although full time advocacy does not mix well with trying to run a busy office and going in and out of police stations at strange hours of the night. There will be economic pressure to start conducting serious trials before the advocate feels ready, whether they are prosecuting or defending.

One of the most important tasks with the serious cases, like drug importation or causing death by dangerous driving, is putting the evidence together, making sure that the pieces of the jigsaw fit, finding out where the weak points are and whether the holes can be plugged. It is very beneficial to have a second pair of eyes then scrutinising what has been prepared. I have often been very grateful to counsel for pointing out the gaps in the evidence which I had missed, and it will indeed be a loss to the profession if the independent Bar is damaged by the so-called reforms.

So much for the doom and gloom. You have joined a truly great profession and you can look forward to fellowship and warmth from many of your colleagues. Provided you are interested in people, you will never be bored. Defendants will surprise you. You will meet people who have had the most appalling lives who somehow have managed to retain a basic decency and others who have had every advantage in their families and education who have nevertheless gone off the rails. You will meet some people who have blundered into a criminal lifestyle almost by mistake and a few who are quite simply wicked.

May your pen never run dry, your voice and your courage never fail you and your gown never go missing! And above all, may you survive meeting the lions.

Useful Websites

www.opsi.gov.uk/acts.htm
Gives access to Acts of Parliament for 1972 and 1988 onwards. Scroll down the screen to Public Acts, click your mouse on the relevant year and you will then find an alphabetical list of the Acts of Parliament.

www.publications.parliament.uk/pa/pabills.htm
This will give you details of legislation going through at present.

www.bailii.org, www.lawreports.co.uk,
www.hmcourts-service.gov.uk/cms/judgments.htm
These sites provide free case reports. There are other websites, such as Lawtel or Westlaw, but they are not cheap if you are paying out of your own pocket.

www.sentencing-guidelines.gov.uk
The website of the Sentencing Guidelines Council. There is a useful compendium of significant reported cases in the Court of Appeal guidelines section. There is also a section of 'Useful Links', which will connect you to websites for ACPO (Association of Chief Police Officers), the Probation service and the CPS.

www.hmprisonservice.gov.uk
Useful when you have a conference arranged at a distant prison and you have no idea where you are going. You can locate any prison on this site; clicking on 'Visitor Information' will tell you how to get there.

www.legalservices.gov.uk

The Legal Services Commission will tell you about the so-called 'reform' of legal aid. Do not open if you are already feeling depressed.

www.clsa.co.uk

The Criminal Law Solicitors Association website. If you are a solicitor you would be wise to join the Association. Its annual conference, once described by its former chairman Judith Naylor as "an annual booze and a whinge", is as genial a gathering of criminal hacks as you are ever likely to encounter and provides much needed CPD points.

www.inspectorates.homeoffice.gov.uk/hmic

Will give you access to the reports of Her Majesty's Inspectorate of Constabulary. The report into rape prosecutions *Without Consent*, 2007, may be of particular interest.

www.justice.gov.uk/criminal/procrules_fin/index.htm

The Criminal Procedure Rules, includes forms for all occasions, useful for Bad Character, Hearsay and Special Measures applications.

www.courtserve2.net/court-lists.htm

For access to daily court lists (It won't let you into the weekly lists unless you are paying!)

www.thedx.co.uk

Enables you to search the DX to find a subscriber.

www.streeetmap.co.uk

Enables you to find a place provided you have the post code (useful for getting to strange courts or to conferences in strange offices).

www.nationalrail.co.uk
For railway timetables

www.crimeline.info/joomlasite
An excellent weekly update with case reports, details of which sections of statutes are coming into force, topical press reports. Free, and everyone is reading it. Sign up and it will be in your 'inbox' regularly.

www.sacredspace.ie
For some space when you are feeling stressed.

Appendix II

Bad Character Applications

Bad character is dealt with in Sections 98-113 of the Criminal Justice Act 2003. Changes to the rules can be found in the Criminal Justice Act 2003.

What is bad character? s.98

'evidence of, or of a disposition towards, misconduct on his part', other than evidence concerning the charge the defendant is currently facing.

s.101 Evidence of a Defendant's bad character can be given if

- the Defence and the Prosecution agree;

- the Defendant decides to give the evidence himself. A defendant may decide he wants to tell the jury all about his past – "I know I did all these shopliftings but I am not a burglar".

- it is important 'explanatory evidence', i.e. you can better understand what is happening if you know about it.

- it is relevant to a matter in issue between the Defence and the Prosecution – This includes (s.103) where the Prosecution say he has a 'propensity to commit the offence'. Examples would be people who cannot stop hitting their wives/girlfriends/ boyfriends etc.; people who have a raging drug addiction; people who just will not stop burgling houses. But there have to be convictions for the same type of offences. A person who goes out shoplifting is not necessarily the same person who gets into fights in his local pub. 'Propensity' is what is most usually argued in order to admit previous convictions.

There is a Schedule in the Criminal Justice Act of offences which can be classed as similar.

- matter in issue between a defendant and a co-defendant.

- evidence to correct a false impression. Where the convictions should go in because the Defendant is trying to give the court a false impression about himself. For example, he tries to give the impression that he has not been in trouble before when he has. This can include what he says when interviewed by the police under caution.

  A Defendant may be giving a false impression by his 'conduct' – which s.105 says can include 'appearance or dress'. So if he turns up in a dog collar when he has never been to church in his life, his convictions might go in. Should prosecutors be seeking to put in convictions of people who wash and turn up in a suit?

- if he makes an attack on the character of another person. See s.106. This is very similar to what has previously always been the situation. For example, if a Defendant alleged that the police were maliciously making up a story, his convictions went in. The difference is that now the court can also look at anything he says in his interview to see if he makes that sort of allegation.

What to look for?

Convictions that are of a similar type to the one which you are dealing with. The more the better from the Prosecution point of view, and they need to be recent unless they are particularly serious. For example, a conviction for rape of a child might well be admitted even though it was years old, while no one is going to be interested in a shoplifting conviction from ten years ago.

Too much enthusiasm from prosecutors can lead to disappointment – convictions have to be very similar and the judge has to agree it is right to let them in. Just having a list will not be sufficient. It will usually be necessary to have retrieved old files from storage and to have the facts of the cases. Read the Court of Appeal cases considered together of <u>R v. Hanson</u>, <u>R v. Gilmore</u>, <u>R. v P</u> (2005) which give detailed guidance.

Whether or not fixed penalty notices or cautions should be let in has been much discussed. A defendant may well have accepted one of these rather than take the risk and trouble of going to court and disputing the facts of what the Prosecution are seeking to admit.

Emergency Guide to the Hearsay Provisions

Set out in Criminal Justice Act 2003

First rule of survival – do not panic!
The provisions on hearsay are not as radical or as scary as we might think. The legislation does not look all that difficult!

What is hearsay?
"…an assertion other than one made by a person while giving oral evidence" (from the judgement in Sharp (1988)), e.g. second hand gossip.

Hearsay can be admitted if all parties agree.
This most often arises in medical reports, or there are circumstances in which both parties will agree to let the Bench see a custody record, rather than having to call the custody sergeant.

Basically the court will look at all the circumstances before deciding to let in hearsay evidence in the form of documents and consider whether it would be fair to let it in. It is all similar to the pre-existing provisions for reading the statements of witnesses who are too frightened to attend.

See s.114
This sets out the factors to be considered: basically, the importance of the evidence to the case, the circumstances and why hearsay evidence is being produced, "..whether oral evidence can be given" and if not why not. The more central the evidence to the case the less likely the court is to let it in, because of the unfairness caused by not being able to cross-examine.

s.115

The new provisions expressly cover photofits, pictures generally and sketches.

What happens when a witness becomes unavailable is covered by s.116 – one of 5 conditions has to be satisfied. The witness has to be:

- dead; or
- unfit on health grounds (physical or mental);
- outside the UK and it is not practicable for him to be called;
- can't be found – but reasonable steps to find the person must have been taken;
- absent through fear.

'Fear' is to be construed widely, and includes fear of financial loss. If the person is unavailable due to something done by the person for whom he is being called, or by someone acting for that person, then the evidence can't go in. This covers a defendant deliberately trying to keep a witness away because of not wanting the person to be cross-examined!

Evidence from a police officer or other responsible person who has had contact with the witness will be expected if an application on grounds of 'fear' is to succeed.

When deciding to let the evidence in, the court has to consider whether it would be fair, and should also consider whether granting special measures could solve the problem. There are some people who will be prepared to give evidence from behind a screen, but not if they have to face the defendant across a crowded court room.

Often it is not the thought of the court room which causes the fear: it is the worry about being attacked by the defendant's friends and relations afterwards.

s.117

This section covers business records. Very similar to s.24 of the Criminal Justice Act 1988, which it replaces. Records kept in the course of a business are admissible, but general principles apply and the information has to be reliable. The person who makes the statement should be an employee or someone acting in the course of a business, trade or profession and it should be possible to show the chain of how the record that is being used has been created.

s.118

Preserves certain existing rules. Maps, birth, death and marriage certificates, court records. Res gestae is still preserved (e.g. statements made by a person who is dying, or by a witness in the middle of a traumatic experience), confessions made to the police, statements made by people in a common enterprise (e.g. conspiracy), expert evidence (doctors and others giving their professional opinion based on their professional knowledge).

s.119

Where a person gives evidence in person and admits having made a statement previously which is not the same as what he has said in the witness box, the previous statement can be used and can be accepted as good evidence by the court. (n.b. This does not mean that the court has to believe it.)

s.120

Where a witness has been cross-examined on a previous statement, the statement itself can be admissible evidence provided that:

- he agrees that he made the statement;
- to the best of his belief the statement is true.

And also provided that either:

- the statement describes or identifies a person, object or place (i.e. does not just express an opinion);
- or the statement was made when he could remember what had happened and he can't reasonably be expected to remember now;
- or he is the aggrieved and the statement is a complaint made as soon as he could.

This section will help where witnesses cannot remember and will get in recent complaints on assaults and affrays, as well as for sex offences.

Supplementary sections

These deal with safeguards. Anyone making a statement has to understand what he/she is doing, the credibility of a witness who has not given oral evidence can be challenged and if the hearsay evidence is unconvincing the judge can stop the trial and tell the jury to acquit.

Under s.126 a judge has the power to refuse to admit a statement if he thinks that letting it in "would result in undue waste of time.... taking account of the value of the evidence."

s.127

Deals with expert evidence and preparatory work: it should now be possible to put in drugs analysis with fewer problems.

s.128

A confession by someone accused may be used by a co-accused. (Sadly, it does not look as if we can use confessions by one person to prove the case against another.)

Notices should be served, but the Court can agree to dispense with them.

If you are in doubt about whether a Notice is required for a particular piece of evidence, it would be sensible to raise this as a query with the judge at the Plea and Case Management Hearing or with the court clerk at a pre-trial review hearing in the magistrates court. When these provisions first came in, it was thought necessary in some areas for notices to be served even for records of the defendant's interview and for statements like medical evidence which had been admitted as a matter of course previously. Fortunately, common sense now seems to prevail and it could be said that the Defence by admitting that some evidence can be read Section 9 without the witness attending, have agreed to the hearsay evidence being given. But check to be safe. Beware particularly of medical reports which have opinions in them about causation of injuries as well as details of matters like how many stitches were needed to close a wound.

About Carbolic Smoke Ball Co.

The Carbolic Smoke Ball Co. is named after the famous law case of 1892, *Carlill v. Carbolic Smoke Ball Co.,* which clarified the important principle of offer and consideration in contract law.

Our namesake went into liquidation in 1893, shortly after the Court of Appeal decided that the company's offer of £100 to anyone who used its patented smoke ball yet contracted influenza was an offer that had to be honoured and not a 'mere puff'. For the last 15 years, we have avoided that fate, selling a wide variety of law-themed stationery and gifts to solicitors and barristers worldwide. Our website is at:

> www.carbolicsmokeball.com

There you will find:

- 20 of the best law cartoons from the *Punch* archives, available framed, for your office wall.
- A wide selection of classic law pictures, including Vanity Fair, law buildings, the Inns of Court etc.
- Cufflinks, bracelets, necklaces and earrings bearing legal motifs.
- Ties, t-shirts and sweatshirts with legal slogans.
- Lawyer's Christmas and greetings cards.
- Coffee mugs, coasters and paperweights.
- Gavels, lecterns, wig boxes, and other accessories.
- Hundred of other law-themed products . . .

Carbolic Smoke Ball Co. – Contact Details

If you would like a copy of the latest Carbolic Smoke Ball Co. catalogue, or want to get in touch with us for any other reason, please contact us by one of these means:

Phone: 01252 795951

Fax: 01252 790777

Email: enquiries@carbolicsmokeball.com

Post: Carbolic Smoke Ball Co.
Silverbeck
Jumps Road
Churt
Farnham
Surrey
GU10 2HL